The Illuminati Wealth Society

The Not-Get-Rich-Quick Scheme

AF730928

(Principles to help you achieve more success, abundance, and fulfillment in your business & your life)

David Paul Coker
Founder of "The Illuminati Wealth Society"

"I'm hoping you find this book to be just the right mix of get-rich-quick schemes, not-get-rich-quick schemes, and the foundations for building wealth and a wealthy-thinking mindset! Do I have your attention?"

The Illuminati Wealth Society

Copyright Page

© 2020 Coker Financial Investments, LLC

First Edition Paperback 2020

ISBN-13: 978-1-7344582-1-3

All rights reserved. This book or parts thereof may not be reproduced in any form, stored in any retrieval system, or transmitted in any form by any means—electronic, mechanical, photocopy, recording, or otherwise—without prior written permission of the publisher, except as provided by United States of America copyright law. For permission requests, write to the publisher, at "Attention: Permissions Coordinator," at the address below.

Coker Financial Investments, LLC acting as publisher
757 SE 17th Street, #281
Fort Lauderdale, FL 33316
https://illuminatiwealthsociety.com
websupport@illuminatiwealthsociety.com

The Illuminati Wealth Society name, images, graphics, and logo are trademarks belonging to Coker Financial Investments, LLC.

To find out more about The IWS and the author, David Paul Coker, visit our website at https://illuminatiwealthsociety.com

Legal Disclaimer

The Illuminati Wealth Society, this book, and the content provided herein are simply for entertainment purposes, educational purposes, and general guidance; and do not take the place of legal advice from your attorney, accounting advice from your Accountant, or investment advice from your Investment Advisor. Every effort has been made to ensure that the content provided in this book is accurate and helpful for our readers at publishing time. However, this is not an exhaustive treatment of the subjects. No liability is assumed for losses or damages due to the information provided. You are responsible for your own choices, actions, decisions, and results.

Further, this book is not intended as a substitute for the medical advice of a physician. The reader should regularly consult a physician in matters relating to his/her health and particularly with respect to any symptoms that may require diagnosis or medical attention.

Illuminati Disclaimer

The Illuminati Wealth Society is not a religion or a cult. We are not connected to the Bavarian Illuminati or what the mainstream media would refer to as the "Modern Day" Illuminati. We aren't part of some dark and sinister plot of world domination either, but rather we are part of a movement promoting individual self-empowerment and self-improvement. We are a new kind of illumination, enlightenment, mindset, and thinking with a purpose of promoting success, abundance, and fulfillment in businesses and life. We can be thought of as a group, club, organization, fraternity, or society of like-minded individuals with that as our common purpose. We are not the illuminati, but rather we are, The Illuminati Wealth Society!

Table of Contents

Introduction

"The things that will destroy America are prosperity-at-any-price, peace-at-any-price, safety-first instead of duty-first, the love of soft living, and the get-rich-quick theory of life."[1]

Over the last several months, during all of my spare time away from work, I had been reading and thinking a great deal about the subjects of wealth, riches, and goals; along with the ideas and concepts of success, abundance, and fulfillment. Then one morning, something interesting happened.

I woke up at about 5:30am that morning and the majority of this idea and information came into my mind via a lucid dream and I was inspired to start writing it down upon my awakening. An hour and a half later I had written the basis of what had come into my mind...as a result, the existence of this little book, "The Not-Get-Rich-Quick Scheme" was born and came into existence.

[1] Theodore Roosevelt Quotes. BrainyQuote.com, Xplore Inc, 2018. https://www.brainyquote.com/quotes/theodore_roosevelt_164291, accessed July 18, 2018. Roosevelt was a statesmen and writer who served as the 26th President of The United States from 1901-1909.

For me it felt like a flash of inspiration or a moment of clarity during that lucid dream. Whether it really was remains to be seen and as similar to beauty, perhaps it will only ever be in the eye of the beholder, but I digress. My hope is that it can help a few people to improve their life and that I can have the strength and discipline to use it to help improve my own life as well.

The Not-Get-Rich-Quick Scheme.

What is the best way to get rich? Quickly, surely, or smartly? After reading this book, the answer should be quite clear and hopefully you will be inspired to act toward building your own personal life of wealth and riches that most people only dream about.

Figure 1 – For you, a life of wealth and riches that most people only dream about is becoming more of a reality every day!

In the next section, I give a little background info about me just so that you can know a little more about me and who I am.

About Me: David Paul Coker

About me, and the passion I have for more success, abundance, and fulfillment in business and life.

I know that if I can help enough other people get what they want in life, I will be rewarded with everything I want in life as well. If I can help enough other people have more success, abundance, and fulfillment in their lives, I will have more success, abundance, and fulfillment in my life as well.

I'm the founder of The Illuminati Wealth Society (IWS). We are a society of like-minded individuals that realize we are in control of our own lives and are directing them to achieve more success, abundance, and fulfillment. The Illuminati Wealth Society is a division and brand of Coker Financial Investments, LLC, which is my consulting business.

I accept the challenge to be your guide, trusted advisor, coach, champion, and friend on this journey to help you have more success, abundance, and fulfillment in business and life!

I received my Bachelor's Degree in Business Administration with a major in Accounting from The University of South Carolina - Darla Moore School of Business. I've always been passionate about understanding the principles of how money works and investing.

I'm a Certified Internal Auditor (CIA). This means I specialized within the accounting profession to serve the shareholders, audit committee, board of directors, executive management, internal audit management, and operations management by understanding, consulting, and testing financial processes, internal controls, the financial reporting structure, and safeguarding of assets within a corporate business environment.

I have more than 18 years of accounting / auditing experience for various different companies.

A few companies I've worked for include: HEICO Corporation, The Siegfried Group, Price Waterhouse Coopers, Tenet Health System, Arthur Andersen, Blue Cross Blue Shield, and United Parcel Service (UPS).

At this point I've read more than 60 Books in just the last few years on topics such as business, investing, wealth, taxes, goals, success, self-improvement, history, philosophy, and other topics to further prepare me for this journey. I do my best to keep an updated list, just in case family or friends might want to see the input that went into my mind over the last few years. Also, I can go back to my list and think about what I learned from a particular book.

I have certifications in Business Coaching, Life Coaching, and Time Management.

I've been sharing knowledge and advice with my closest friends for several years to help them have more success, abundance, and fulfilment. Now I want to serve you in your quest and adventure for more success, abundance, and fulfillment in business & life too!

The Illuminati Wealth Society and its products and services are a brand of and provided through Coker Financial Investments, LLC.

Walking through the castle at Carcassonne, France.

On a ship enjoying the ocean breeze and last bit of sunlight for the day.

Body

A get-rich-quick scheme is a grand, too-good-to-be-true idea often sold by a con man to an uninformed, uneducated, or inexperienced investor that promises high rates of return over a short period of time with minimal risk. The term "get-rich-quick" seems to have been in use since at least the early 1900's[2] to describe unregulated, fake, or shady-natured investments.

Stepping back for a moment, from the author, entrepreneur, philanthropist, and life coach Anthony "Tony" Robbins; I learned that being "wealthy" is a state of mind; however, being "rich" is a monetary goal that you have set for yourself and achieved. That is something to keep in mind as we work on improving our wealthy-thinking-mindset and accomplish our goals to attain the riches we seek and desire.

Here's the thing though. Wealth and riches are connected because wealth can make you feel rich, and riches (income) can enhance your wealth; therefore, they complement each other nicely. Put another way,

[2] The "Blockite" and the "Get-rich-quick Man" by S.A. Nelson. Everybody's Magazine, vol 10, 1904.

you can have all the riches you desire, but without a wealthy-thinking-mindset you probably won't be very happy because you'll be trying to get your meaning in life primarily from money and material things themselves. How do you know if you are wealthy? Well if your money is causing you to lack having a major purpose in life or overindulge in your vices, then you got some work to do as you are being controlled by a poor-thinking-mindset. If money is enhancing your ability and allowing you to act in a positive manner toward your self-determined purpose in life, you very likely are going to feel wealthy and most likely on the right path in life to not only building and maintaining your wealth, but also having more success, abundance, and fulfillment; along with more happiness and better health as well.

Some people will see the book's title or first few lines and not be interested, some people will read this and not understand the message being placed before them, but some of you will approach this with an open mind, understand the meaning of what is being expressed in this book and will be inspired to act toward something positive and wonderful. After reading "The Not-Get-Rich-Quick Scheme", some of you may feel cheated or even laugh. However, others of you will understand completely and totally get it, will be thankful you read this book, and will use it to help transform your life in the here and now; thus, altering your future life trajectory to a higher plane of wealth and riches.

Why are people poor? Generally, it stems from a poor-thinking-mindset of negative actions and lack of positive actions. The cause of a poor-thinking-mindset has the effect of making a person become and remain poor. Of course, going along with that, a person can become poor because of oppression, circumstances, or choices. Oppression and circumstances are difficult to change, unless you can move to a part of the world with freedom and better circumstances or improve those things where you currently live. Choices on the other hand, are more within our control and it's relatively easy to start making better choices in life.

In a study by the Community Empowerment Collective (C.E.C.) and by my own observations, I came to learn and realize the root causes of poverty for nearly everyone living below the poverty line on a continuous basis, almost always had one or more combinations of the following 5 things negatively impacting their lives:

1. *Lack of education, knowledge, and understanding.*

- *The poor-thinking mindset person doesn't know and understand how money works. They don't know how to earn it, accumulate it, save it, increase it, compound it, invest it, manage it, and use it wisely.*
- *The poor-thinking mindset person doesn't have skills, products, or services that make them valuable to society and their fellow man. If someone can't provide a skill, service, or a product to better the lives of their fellow man, they will have difficulty in earning income.*
- *The poor-thinking mindset person doesn't understand how the universe works and that it is governed and influenced by the physical natural laws of the universe, the spiritual laws of the universe, and the man-made laws of society as well.*
- *The poor-thinking mindset person doesn't realize they are in control of their own life and can direct it to anything they desire.*

2. *Dependence.*
   - *The poor-thinking mindset person doesn't have income derived from their own thoughts, ideas, labor, actions, and efforts.*
   - *The poor-thinking mindset person continuously takes aide from the government and feels*

entitled to it over the long-term without even taking actions to improve themselves.

- The poor-thinking mindset person continuously depends on charity and taking from others over the long-term in order to survive.

3. Dishonesty.
    - The poor-thinking mindset person doesn't have values.
    - The poor-thinking mindset person doesn't keep their word.
    - The poor-thinking mindset person can't be trusted to act with integrity.
    - The poor-thinking mindset person doesn't see that fair dealings with others can be a win-win situation where it benefits both sides.

4. Disease.
    - Diseases can take many forms. Diseases can be physical, mental, or emotional. The word disease means, "without ease". It is the opposite of being at ease.
    - Fear is a disease that can stop you from acting, accomplishing goals, and working toward your dreams. If you are scared to fly, you will never see the world. If you fear talking to someone you are attracted to, you may never fall in-love. If you fear public speaking, your career will suffer and you may

never achieve your fullest potential to help others through yours or your employer's products and services.

- *Once someone is addicted to drugs or alcohol, they have a huge problem in life. Because of this disease, they only care about feeding their addiction. Their relationships, health, work, income, wealth, and well-being start to become neglected and suffer. Often times an addict cannot and will not recognize or admit they have a problem. Everything and everyone around them will be brought down and eventually their family and friends will even be pushed away so much so that the person can become homeless as they use every bit of their resources, time, and efforts to feed the addiction.*

5. *Apathy.*
    - *The poor-thinking mindset person has no purpose or goals in life. They are drifting aimlessly. Life is just happening to them, instead of them taking massive action and creating the life they want.*
    - *If you aren't acting toward what you want in life, you aren't growing. If you aren't growing, you aren't improving and becoming better.*
    - *The poor-thinking mindset person doesn't care what happens to themselves, their family, their*

fellow man, or the world in general; therefore, they probably won't be motivated to do anything positive and constructive with their life or to improve the life of others.

Any one of these causes being present in someone's life can be disastrous and cause them to fall into poverty. If someone has multiple root causes present in their life, they have an even greater chance of falling into poverty and remaining there. Within these root causes there are many different specific stories and examples that can lead to poverty, but a common thread here in these things is they are all within our control and we can overcome them by changing who we are and what we do in our life.

We can remove all of these factors from our life by making a choice and taking massive action. Understand that you are the creator of your life. It should make sense if you remove these root causes of poverty from your life and start to do the opposite of them, they can lead to wealth, riches, and your dreams coming true. You can start to turn these root causes of poverty into the root causes of wealth. Taking the opposite of the root causes of poverty, we can turn them into the root causes of wealth, such as:

- *The wealthy-thinking-mindset person is motivated, takes action, and works toward increasing their knowledge, wisdom, and understanding about the universe, about life, about themselves, about their fellow man, about money, about business, and about a number of many other topics. Further, we are serving our fellow man by having a skill, trade, craft, profession, product, service, or art that provides value to the market. We are also doing our best to be in-tune with the physical laws of the universe, natural laws of the universe, and the man-made laws of society. Money and income are earned by our quality of work, our quantity of work, and our mental attitude. Increase any one of these three things and our earning power will increase. Increase all three, and our earning power can and should increase exponentially.*
- *The wealthy-thinking-mindset person works to achieve independence. Our income and wealth are derived from the fruits of our own efforts in conjunction with serving our fellow man.*
- *The wealthy-thinking-mindset person is known for their honesty. We have integrity*

in what we say, what we do, and who we are. People can count on us to keep our word. Our word is our bond.

- *The wealthy-thinking-mindset person is the master of their domain. We control our vices instead of our vices controlling us. We strive to be positive and open-minded. We know, accept, and understand we are in control of our life and can direct it to anything we desire. We develop and maintain an attitude of gratitude and a positive mental attitude toward all we get to do in life.*
- *The wealthy-thinking-mindset person cares about and takes massive action toward what they see as important in their life. We set and achieve our goals. Do your best to start caring about yourself, have love for yourself, choose your financial future, and do that for others around you as well.*

It can be easy to fall prey to a get-rich-quick scheme or be taken by a slick, unethical salesmen as history can show us over the years. You may have already heard the stories I'm about to mention, but I think they bare repeating if they can help us to keep our money and help us choose wise investments. Here are few of the most notorious "Get-rich-quick" schemes of all time:

Figure 2 - Water color painting of a tulip. The beautiful tulip was a luxury, but also a commodity or investment in 17th century Europe.

Tulip mania - Today the term is sometimes used metaphorically to describe an inflated economic bubble where asset prices are greatly diverging from their true inherent fundamental values. The Dutch "Tulip Mania" in the winter of 1637 occurred when the price of tulips and the futures contracts associated with them collapsed after the prices had previously gone parabolic in the time leading up to the collapse. Futures markets appeared in Europe in the 1600's and tulips were widely traded and speculated upon in the years leading up to the collapse. At one point, a single highly prized tulip could sell for as much as 10 times the average worker's annual earnings. They were a highly sought-after luxury item as some parts of Europe were experiencing a "Golden Age" and doing quite well. Speculators were buying and selling futures contracts, without the actual tulips ever even changing hands, in the hopes of making quick money and becoming rich. As with any asset bubble, buying eventually dries up as the prices are seen to be too expensive for new buyers or some new event changes the dynamics of the market. The parabolic price increase in tulips showed that a "mania" was clearly underway; however, speculators refused to see it. There is some speculation about a few other factors that burst the bubble as well. For example, parts of Europe, including The Netherlands, were experiencing the epidemic of bubonic plague, which ravaged much of Europe.

Also, the Futures Contracts were not highly regulated. They were traded in taverns and bars vs. being traded on a regulated exchange. Further, the government had made a change, which allowed speculators to cancel their contracts with only having to a pay a 10% penalty fee. All of these factors and other variables created the perfect storm, which allowed the tulip prices to have a parabolic price increase and then a dramatic bursting of the bubble where tulip prices plummeted. Just as with any pyramid scheme, fortunes can be made early on, but those showing up late to the party, are often left holding the empty bag, and lose their money. What happened during the Tulip Mania can be further illustrated by The Greater Fool Economic Theory, which says the price of something is not decided by intrinsic value alone, but instead by illogical & unreasonable opinions and hopes of market participants. A price can be justified by a logical and reasonable buyer if they think another party will pay even higher prices. Meaning, someone may pay a ridiculously foolish price because they believe the object can be sold to a "greater fool" in the future. Similar to the tulip mania, in 2018 this seemed to be playing out with the irrational exuberant price and subsequent crash of Bitcoin and other cryptocurrencies as well. It will be interesting to keep an eye on Bitcoin and the other cryptocurrencies to see where things go in the future.

Figure 3 - Many a con man has used the Ponzi Scheme or Pyramid Scheme to defraud innocent people. If it sounds too good to be true, it probably is not true!

Figure 4 - Images reminiscent of the products pushed by the snake oil salesman of the late 19th and early 20th centuries when pharma was not regulated.

The Snake Oil Salesmen - Often thought of as a con man, hustler, or charlatan. In the late 19th and early 20th century, these Snake Oil Salesmen could be seen in the streets pushing their inferior goods or fake medicine via various bottled elixirs or tonics. During that era, medicine was not highly regulated, thus these con men seized on the opportunity to sell an unsubstantiated and unregulated product to gullible buyers. The prevailing thought of the day was "caveat emptor", also known as, "let the buyer beware".

Meaning if you don't do your research, homework, and understand what you are buying; you are very likely to get what you deserve, shoddy and inferior products or medicines. It is interesting that some material I've seen preparing for this topic pointed out that including Omega-3 fatty acids in your diet has some positive health benefits; however, the actual benefits of taking Omega-3 fish oil supplements is difficult to confirm, thus some bring up the point that Fish Oil supplements and some other vitamins may just be the modern-day version of the Snake Oil Salesman's elixirs and tonics. I think it's something interesting you could ponder and do more research on and draw your own conclusions. For a normal, relatively healthy person, it seems to me that good high-quality food promotes a healthy body the best; however, in the end, you have to do what is right for you.

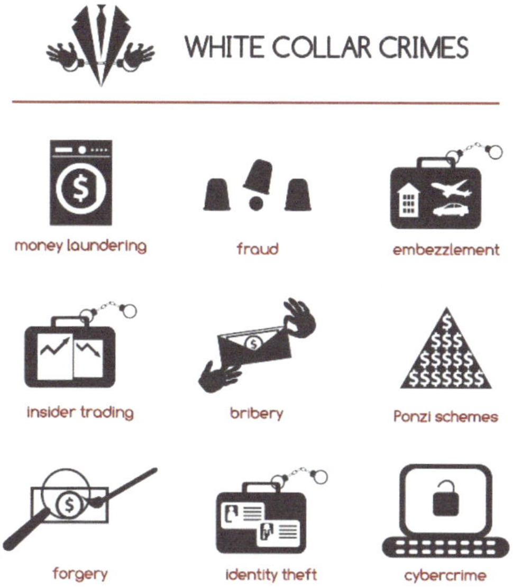

Figure 5 - The more you know about and understand these white-collar crimes, the better prepared you will be to spot them and not fall victim to them either.

Charles Ponzi - born Carlo Pietro Giovanni Guglielmo Tebaldo Ponzi lived 1882 - 1949 was a financier and fraudster in Boston whose name and actions are the basis for what is now called the "Ponzi scheme". He promised investors he would double their money in 90 days via a complex and difficult to explain and understand arbitrage plan where he would buy and resell international postal-reply coupons; however, according to the post office, these coupons could not actually be redeemed for cash money and this fact was hidden from the investors. Ponzi was able to use the scheme to collect around $8 million from about 30,000 investors in less than a year. In essence he was just paying off a few early investors with money that was collected later, so it seemed liked early investors were already making money as he promised. Ponzi was also just spending the collected money as his own. The scheme eventually collapsed and Ponzi was found guilty of forgery, mail fraud, and larceny serving 14 years in prison. He lived the remainder of his life with a meager existence working odd jobs and attempting to run other schemes that never panned out for him. At the age of 66 and in poor health, he died at a charity hospital in Rio de Janeiro, Brazil.

Figure 6 - A fool and his money are soon parted. If you don't know what to do with your money, the worst thing you can do is tell someone you have money. Gain knowledge, wisdom, experience, and find a trusted mentor or advisor. Once you have these things in place, it won't be so easy for someone to cheat you out of your hard-earned money.

Bernard "Bernie" Lawrence Madoff - born 1938 in Queens, New York. His father was a plumber by trade and a stockbroker (interesting combination); and Madoff himself was a stockbroker, investment advisor, and financier that founded Bernard L. Madoff Investment Securities, LLC that started off as a penny stock trading company in 1960. Through the firm, Madoff would convince investors to turn over their money to him where he claimed he would invest it on their behalf. He promised returns that seemed too good to be true. He even produced phony investment statements showing the returns appeared to be achieved and the customer's accounts were growing. Further, the accounting firm Madoff hired to audit his company, was a small unknown accounting firm that was part of the scheme where they would falsify their audit reports so that everything appeared to be legitimate with Madoff and his company. Through the years, there were plenty of red-flags; however, people still kept investing with him based on his name and extraordinary returns he purported to deliver. For years, Madoff just deposited the investor's money into his business account and whenever an investor did request a redemption, he would pay it out of the business account. He also used the money as his own to fund a lavish lifestyle, such as a fleet of yachts, 3 mansion-esque homes, artwork, jewelry, and lavish spending to just name a few things. Eventually, it all caught up with him. In December 2008, when it started to become apparent to many that Madoff was running a Ponzi scheme, Madoff's sons informed the FBI their father had told them the whole thing was a lie. In March 2009, Madoff pleaded guilty to 11 federal felonies and admitted that his wealth management business was nothing more than a Ponzi scheme. It was reported Madoff had defrauded thousands of investors out of somewhere between a net amount of 10 billion to 17 billion dollars. In June of 2009, he was sentenced to 150 years in prison, which was the maximum sentence that could have been imposed, and forfeited nearly 17 billion dollars of assets. At the time of this writing in 2018, Madoff is serving his sentence in Butner Federal Correctional Institution in North Carolina, where he will likely spend the rest of his life.

Try to learn from the above stories and remember their lessons when you are presented with too good to be true investment opportunities or money-making schemes.

Here are some warning signs and red-flags that can help you spot a money scheme or bad investment to stay away from:

- The person running the investment is attempting to obtain money from non-qualified investors. At the time of this writing in 2018, in *general, a qualified investor has an annual income of at least $200,000 in each of the past two years ($300,000 for joint income) or a net worth of at least $1 million). The person running a legitimate investment wouldn't or shouldn't need to encourage an unqualified investor to hand over their hard-earned money. And with a few exceptions, doing so is usually against the law.*

- *The person running the investment has no proven track record of running a business or successfully managing investments.*
- *The person promoting the investment says they are just working for the real people in charge of running the investment and can't provide all the details.*
- *There isn't proper documentation to support the investment. The person promoting or running the investment can't provide a business plan, bank statements, escrow account statements, or financial statements.*
- *The person running the investment and their partners have no experience in relation to what the investment is.*
- *The person running the investment promises extraordinary gains with low or no risk. The*

stock market's long-term return is about 8-10% annually. It's highly unlikely a low risk investment will ever beat that stock market average over the long-term.

- *The person running the investment uses vague concepts or complex scenarios that can't be validated or easily explained and understood.*
- *The person running the investment puts an artificial timeline of urgency for needing to obtain money from you.*
- *You don't understand how the investment will actually generate income or make money.*
- *The investment has too much risk or uncertainty associated with it.*
- *The investment is charging a high management fee. Many financial pundits say anything above 2% annually in management fees is probably unreasonable. In comparison, many profitable and reputable mutual funds or ETF's charge 1% or less in management fees.*

Always review Business Plans, Financial Plans, Annual Reports, SEC filings, and ask management questions whenever you can. If your instincts tell you something doesn't seem right and any of these warning signs or red-flags are present, don't ignore them because they just might save you from making a bad decision and losing your money.

Figure 7 - Review and discuss the business idea and documentation with your business partners, advisors, and mentors. Get their feedback and opinions before making your decision.

What does it take to become rich? Well, we know rich can have many different meanings, thresholds, and mindsets; however, for this example, let's say a net worth above one million dollars. There are 3 general timelines I think about for becoming rich.

1. The surely "Surefire" timeline - earn money, spend less than you earn, save your money, and invest your money. Timeline horizon is 30 years or more. You will have to do things such as:
    - Save 15-20% of your pre-tax income in an IRA or 401k, and invest that money into investments such as stocks, bonds, mutual funds, exchanged traded funds, and possibly even real estate. If you have maxed out your IRA and 401k deductions, you could possibly then save additional amounts into a Roth IRA.
    - Buy a reasonable home, in a good location, at a great price and pay it off in 15 years or as soon as possible. Don't make the bank rich by paying huge sums of interest over a long-term loan if you don't have to. Make yourself rich by paying off your mortgage and avoiding that interest

expense to the bank. Instead of paying extra on the mortgage each month, it can often times work better to save that money into an investment account. Over time those investments will grow. Once they reach enough to pay off the mortgage, you could then just pay it off in one lump sum.

- Buy only used reasonable priced cars.
- Avoid credit card debt.
- Avoid debt on depreciating assets (such as cars and boats).
- Marry a person of integrity with similar values and goals as yourself. Then work together as a team toward your shared and individual goals.

2. The quickly "Get Lucky" timeline – play the lottery, inherit money, win a lawsuit, or marry someone rich. Timeline horizon is today to never. You will have to do things such as:
    - Play the lottery. Odds are not good for winning. It really could be thought of as a "tax" on poor-thinking mindset individuals. But hey, someone has to win. You have the same lousy odds as everyone else.

- *Marry a rich person. You will have to associate with wealthy people. Generally wealthy people only associate with other wealthy people; however, if you are a man or woman of great attractiveness, fame, or charisma, you can often associate with very wealthy individuals. Perhaps you can even convince one of them to marry you one day; however, if you marry only for money, your relationship may never blossom into one of trust, integrity, shared values, common goals, friendship, and love.*

- *Lawsuits. You could make-up a story and sue someone. This is immoral and against the law and you shouldn't do it; however, people do it all the time. I wouldn't want to be that kind of person. However, if you were truly injured through no fault of your own, you may never be the same again, thus society and the justice system may reward you with a monetary settlement. Because of your injuries and loss of income, this money is rightly yours.*

- *Inherit. Maybe you have wealthy grandparents, parents, or aunts and uncles that will look out for you while they are alive or even bequeath part of their estates to you upon their passing into the afterlife. It's sad how many family feuds begin after the passing of a family member over their estate and money. Don't let this happen to you or your family. Make sure you have a will and your heirs understand your last wishes.*
- *The greatest problem with this timeline and the examples above is that you really didn't earn the wealth you received. You can't get and stay wealthy by taking from someone else. Money that is quickly found, is usually quickly lost.*

3. *The smart "Massive Idea-Massive Action" timeline - There a few main ways to make this happen. Here are some massive ideas you can take massive action upon. Provide an above average product or level of service that creates an above average benefit to the market, thus creating an above average income for yourself.*

Purchase real estate at a great value that will appreciate in value over time. You could live in one room and rent out your extra rooms for income to pay down the mortgage faster or use the rental income for additional investing. If you save and invest $70,000 per year and get an 8% return on the investment, you will be a millionaire in about 10 years. How do you live on less and save that much? It won't be easy. Timeline horizon is 10-20 years. You will have to do things such as:

- *See the surely "surefire" timeline mentioned above. Incorporate those strategies into your life along with the strategies mentioned here for the smart "Massive Idea-Massive Action" timeline.*
- *Have a job with a steady paycheck, but also start a business in your spare time.*
- *Write a business plan, start serving your customers, and earn that revenue by providing more value than your competition or customers would expect.*
- *Make the business profitable.*
- *Grow the business. Increase your revenues and net income over time.*

- *After growing the business, have an exit strategy. Sell the business or take it public with an initial public offering.*
- *Be married to a like-minded, supportive, positive spouse with integrity. Be the same back to your spouse. Pool your resources, income, and ideas to make becoming a millionaire a goal and reality.*
- *Share living space and housing costs to reduce expenses. Once you own real estate, you could rent an extra room for income.*
- *Own a very modest car. How modest? If the car is cheap, reliable, and ugly; that's probably the right level of modest in the beginning. Once your income and net worth are more than the average person, you can look at driving nicer vehicles provided your budget allows for it.*
- *Prepare and eat simple meals at home. No visiting expensive restaurants, unless you are working there.*
- *Live a simple life style. Sell anything you don't need.*
- *Buy things on sale.*

- *Buy used whenever possible.*
- *Create a budget and stick to it.*
- *Again, once your income and net worth are on track and greater than the average person, you can start to look at improving your lifestyle. But don't go too crazy. Make sure your lifestyle expenses such as food, restaurants, cars, entertainment, and vacations still make sense in your budget to where you are still saving and investing an acceptable amount of your income.*

Here are some more things to do where you can act immediately and get things going in the right direction.

- *If no income, get a job, take the best thing possible. You need income ASAP! You can drive for a ride-sharing service, deliver pizzas, work at a restaurant, do landscaping, clean homes, be a car salesman, or sell anything you can.*
- *Be grateful and thankful for what you have. Being alive, good health, family, loved-ones, friends, work, income, a place to sleep at night, and the future opportunities you know are*

coming your way. Appreciate and realize how wonderful these things are and how blessed you are to be alive in the here and now.

- Discover your life purpose and how you will use it to serve your fellow man.
- Make a commitment to yourself that you can, will, and must be a better version of your current self; 1 year, 3 years, 5 years, 10 years, 20 years, and 30 years and beyond into the future.
- Invest in yourself. Read books, attend classes, attend seminars, gain valuable work experiences, seek out a mentor to help you master your trade, craft, skills, profession, service, product, and arts.
- Realize how wealthy you are. The best things in life are free and they can be yours. Such as, time, happiness, good health, freedom to be who you are and do what you want to do. Learning new things. Traveling to new places, making new friends, strengthening family and friendship bonds. It's the 2nd best things in life are that are expensive. Such as: cars, boats, big houses, and choosing the wrong spouses.
- Realize a large percentage of people in the world live on the equivalent of less than $3 per day. If you make $100 per day, you are significantly

richer than a large percentage of the world. Hopefully you feel a little more grateful and blessed now.

- Don't live paycheck to paycheck. Reduce your expenses to the bare minimum and if you are in debt, sell all depreciating assets (a.k.a. liabilities) such as: cars, boats, motorcycles, and all expensive toys you don't need. Then use that cash to pay off all debt. Don't take on any new debt. Limit eating out at expensive restaurants. You can eat cheaper, better, and healthier by cooking and eating at home.
- Increase your income. Continue to become a better version of yourself. Offer more value to earn the privilege to receive greater income. Find out exactly what your customer or employer wants and give them even more than that. Once you do, you can raise your prices, apply for new higher positions, ask for a raise, and look for new opportunities that pay more.
- Do a written budget. The more you control your money as opposed to your money controlling you, the richer you will be in everything you do.
- Once you know your monthly expenses, you should still keep improving who you are and how you live your life. This will help with

continuing to improve your income and help you adjust your lifestyle to have living expenses that work well with your budget.

- *In the budget you create for yourself, even after taxes, you should structure your money and life so as to have a budget surplus. Make a designated % of income within your budget to giving. This giving can be to charities, churches, or others. Why? Because helping others makes you rich in spirit and also feel good about who you are. Also, because of the law of attraction what you give out, you will receive back. Further, if you do the giving as part of a charity, group, or organization that you can associate with others and develop friendships, it will be an added benefit. These friendships could even turn to business relationships one day. Also, in a way it prepares you to be an investor by being able to part with your money by putting it into an investment. Both charity and investment provide returns in proportion to your efforts. 10% of your after-tax income to charity has a biblical basis and is a good guide for giving. If you are in debt or don't have your 6-month emergency fund in place yet, I say feel free to adjust down to as low as you feel* *comfortable, say even 1% or even $20 per month. It's your money, but still giving something can have a positive impact on your life and the lives of other. After you're out of debt and have your six-month emergency fund in-place, then you can move it back up to 10% or even higher if your budget allows it. As I said before, you are the steward of the money you have earned and you can choose to do with it as you please. Choose wisely, and you will see and experience the benefits and rewards in your life. Choose poorly, and you will most likely see and experience pain and suffering.*

- *After you've determined taxes and charity within your budget, the next item should be savings. Save something every month, save as much as possible every month, make a goal to get to saving at least 15% of your income every month.*
- *Now that you've reduced expenses, increased your income, created a written budget, know about reducing your tax liability, have a 6-month emergency fund in place, are giving, are saving, are investing, and are no longer living paycheck to paycheck; you should essentially*

have financial security now. You are richer and wealthier than most.

- *Start investing, increase your investing, and get your money to make money for you. When your money makes money for you, yeah now that's cool!*
- *If not already an entrepreneur, start a small business. Anything that will force you to grow as a person and provide you with some additional income.*
- *Join* ***The Illuminati Wealth Society*** *and associate with fellow like-minded members.*
- *Read the other two books in this series of books:*
    - ***The Illuminati Wealth Society*** *- book 2.*
    - ***The Illuminati Wealth Master*** *- book 3.*

Figure 8 - Images portraying King Solomon. King Solomon was the superbly wealthy and wise king of Israel who succeeded his father, King David. The following passage is from, The proverbs of King Solomon in the Holy Bible.

"Wealth from get-rich-quick schemes quickly disappears; wealth from hard work grows over time. Hope deferred makes the heart sick, but a dream fulfilled is a tree of life. People who despise advice are asking for trouble; those who respect a command will succeed. The instruction of the wise is like a life-giving fountain; those who accept it avoid the snares of death. A person with good sense is respected; a treacherous person is headed for destruction. Wise people think before they act; fools don't - and even brag about their foolishness. An unreliable messenger stumbles into trouble, but a reliable messenger brings healing. If you ignore criticism, you will end in poverty and disgrace; if you accept correction, you will be honored."[3]

As we see in the above passage, even The Bible, in the book of Proverbs gives wise advice on the matters of: get-rich-quick schemes, following your dreams, finding wise mentors, taking massive action, and changing who you are and what you do in life, which are all still relevant to this day.

[3] The Holy Bible – Proverbs 13:11-18 (NLT) – The proverbs of King Solomon.

The Bible and many other books are full of great advice and wisdom, but it is up to you to discover, learn, and apply them to your life.

Figure 9 - Do you think they got rich quickly, surely, or smartly??

Conclusion

Do you want to get rich quickly, surely, or smartly? Quickly, the odds are that it will never happen, but you can become rich overnight. Surely, it can take 30 years or more of being disciplined, but you will become wealthy if you follow a good plan. Smartly by itself, isn't guaranteed, but if you follow the plan; along with being an entrepreneur and build up a successful business, run it well, and have a successful exit strategy, it is very possible that within around 10-20 years you can become very wealthy. And don't be dismayed by how long it can take to become wealthy, because I assure you the time is going to pass anyway; so, it mine as well pass while you are working a great plan to become wealthy and having life adventures of your own choosing along the way.

"If you attempt to pursue wealth directly, it will most likely flee from you, and in its place, you will attract a life of difficulty upon yourself; however, if you first seek wisdom, an understanding of wealth, skills or products that are valuable to the market, and provide excellent customer service to others; you will

likely attract wealth into your life, as well as being on the path to more success, abundance, and fulfillment. Since the essence of wealth has a spiritual nature, we cannot just take it from someone, it must be earned by the efforts of our thoughts, ideas, actions, labor, service and wise use of time."[4]

Since you made it this far and are serious about building the life and business of your dreams with more success, abundance, and fulfillment, please take the next step and join,

The Illuminati Wealth Society.

Success, abundance, and fulfillment will soon be yours for all-time!

-David Paul Coker

[4] David Paul Coker, The Illuminati Wealth Society founder

Contact Us

1. If you are interested in joining The Illuminati Wealth Society please visit our website at: *https://IlluminatiWealthSociety.com*

2. If you are interested in Business Coaching, Personal Coaching, Accounting Resourcing, or Financial Education please email us at: *IWS-CoachingConsulting@IlluminatiWealthSociety.com*

3. If **The Illuminati Wealth Society** has helped you have more success, abundance, & fulfillment in your business or life, we would love to hear your story. Maybe after reading our books, joining The IWS, associating with like-minded members of the society, or finding a mentor you accomplished a goal, increased your income and wealth, overcame a fear, improved your relationships, started a business, helped others, or found your definite major purpose in life. Please email us and tell us your story. It would be great to hear from you. Email us at: *IWS-MissionAccomplished@IlluminatiWealthSociety.com*

Made in United States
Troutdale, OR
11/03/2026

56844681R00033